# Doodle Design & Draw CARS

## Steven James Petruccio

**DOVER PUBLICATIONS, INC.**
**Mineola, New York**

Over fifty cool cars inside this book need some finishing touches and cool customizations before they can hit the road. Just grab a pencil and add some sponsor logos to a racecar, draw an exotic car to complete a celebrity's collection, pack the bed of a pick-up truck with all you need for a day at the beach, and much more. Featuring illustrations of sporty, junky, luxury, and other automobiles, future drivers will love testing their skills and creativity with *Doodle, Design & Draw—Cars.*

*Copyright*
Copyright © 2011 by Dover Publications, Inc.
All rights reserved.

*Bibliographical Note*
*Doodle, Design & Draw—Cars* is a new work, first published by
Dover Publications, Inc., in 2011.

*International Standard Book Number*
*ISBN-13: 978-0-486-48055-8*
*ISBN-10: 0-486-48055-0*

Printed in Canada
48055006    2025
www.doverpublications.com

It's time to go for a cool ride in this cool car.
Add some cool wheels and cool graphics to complete the picture.

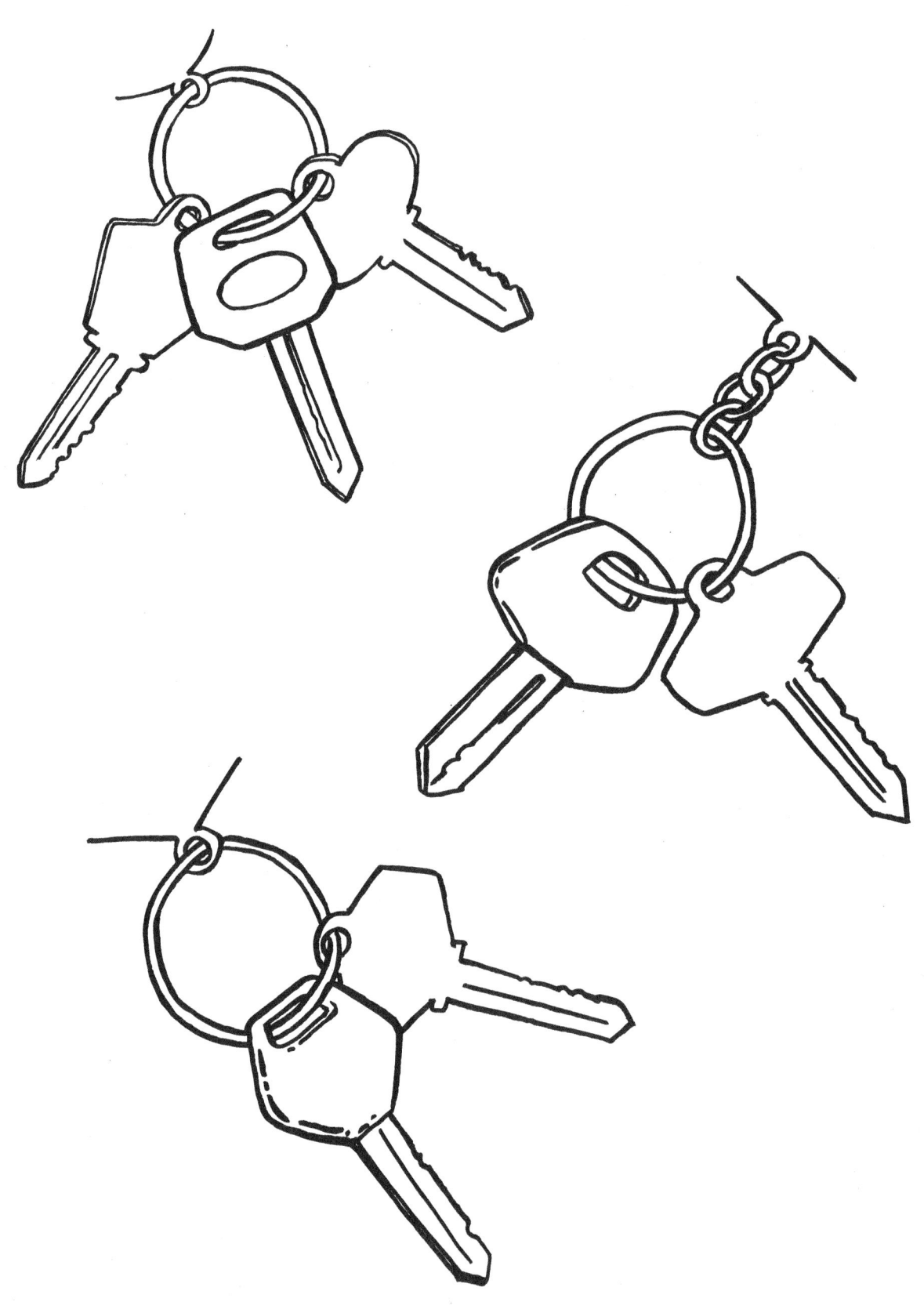

Draw some key chains to hold all these car keys.

Let's go on a road trip! Load the roof with
everything you want to take along.

This car will really bow-wow! Customize it for
the dog-lover and her canine companions.

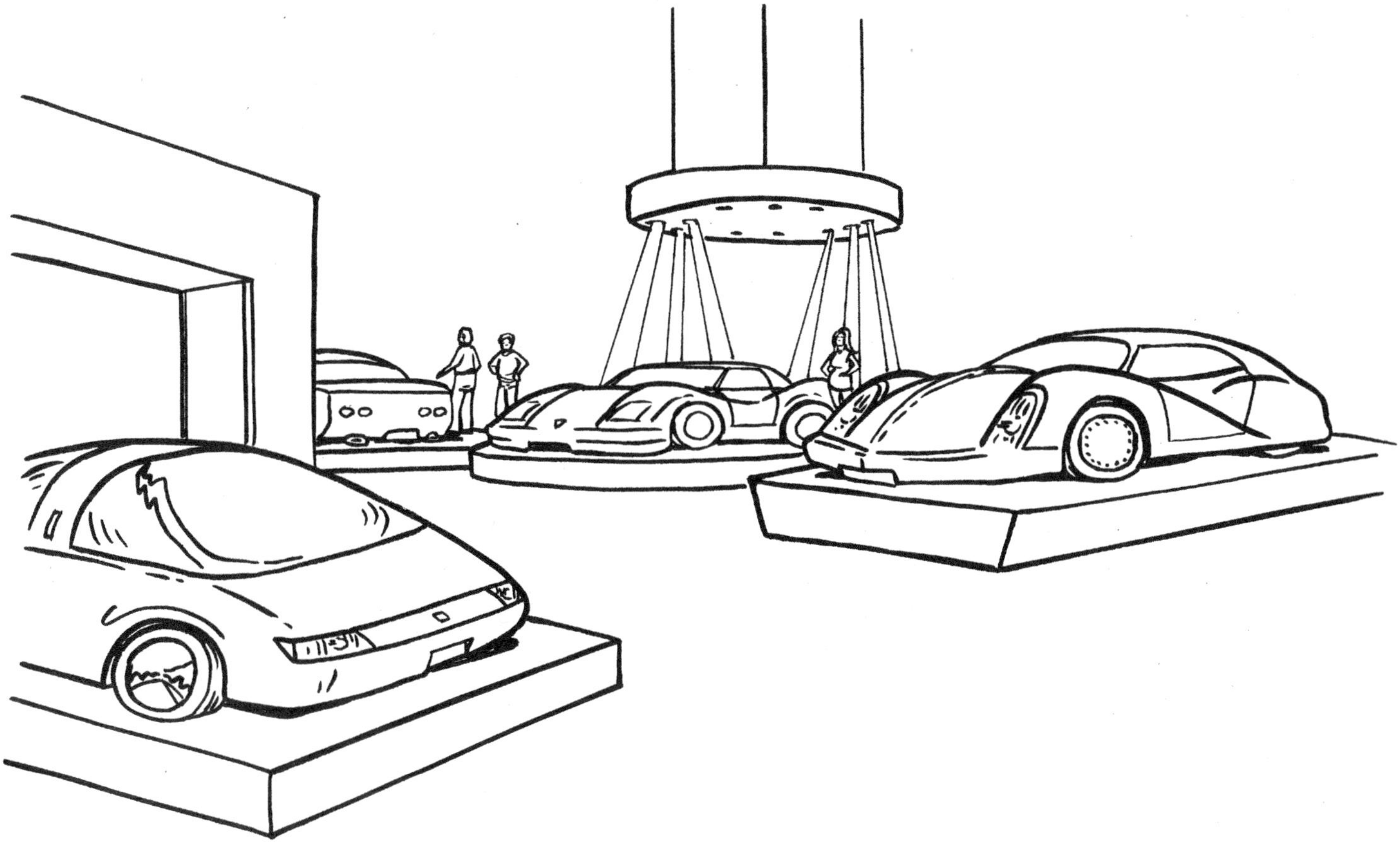

Draw the winner of the first prize ribbon for
"Best New Car" in the Auto Show.

Customize this car so it's really fit for a king!

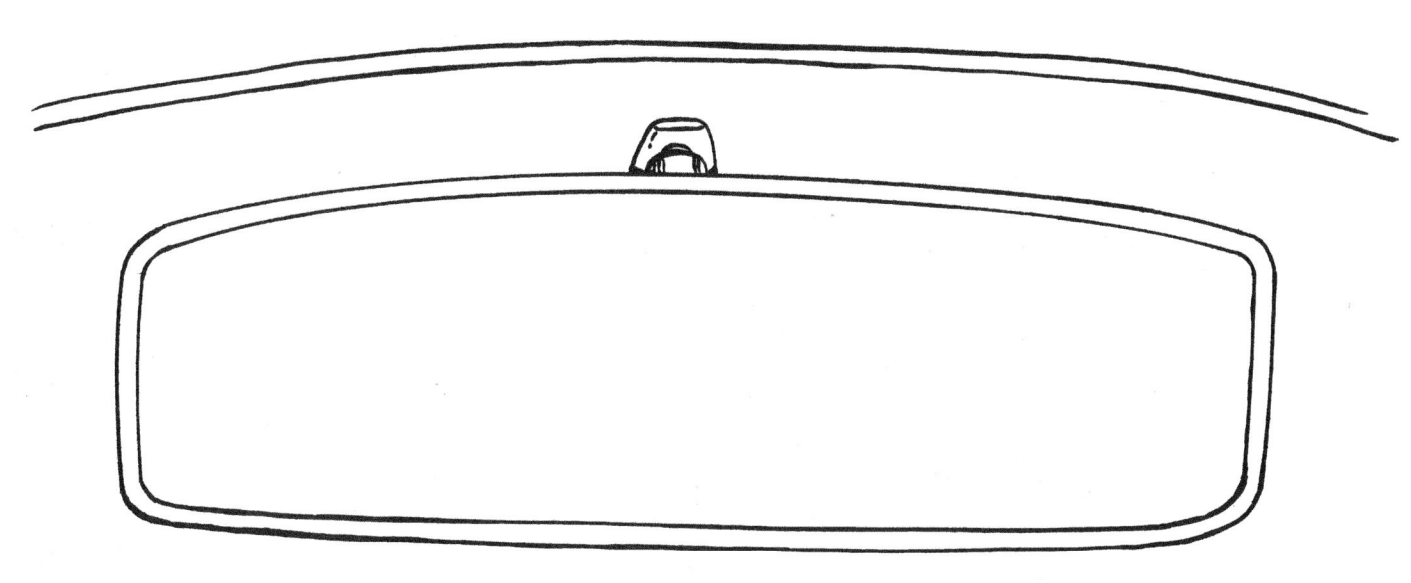

What do you see behind you in the rearview mirror?
What do you see in front of you through the windshield?

The transporter is delivering the latest new cars to your town.

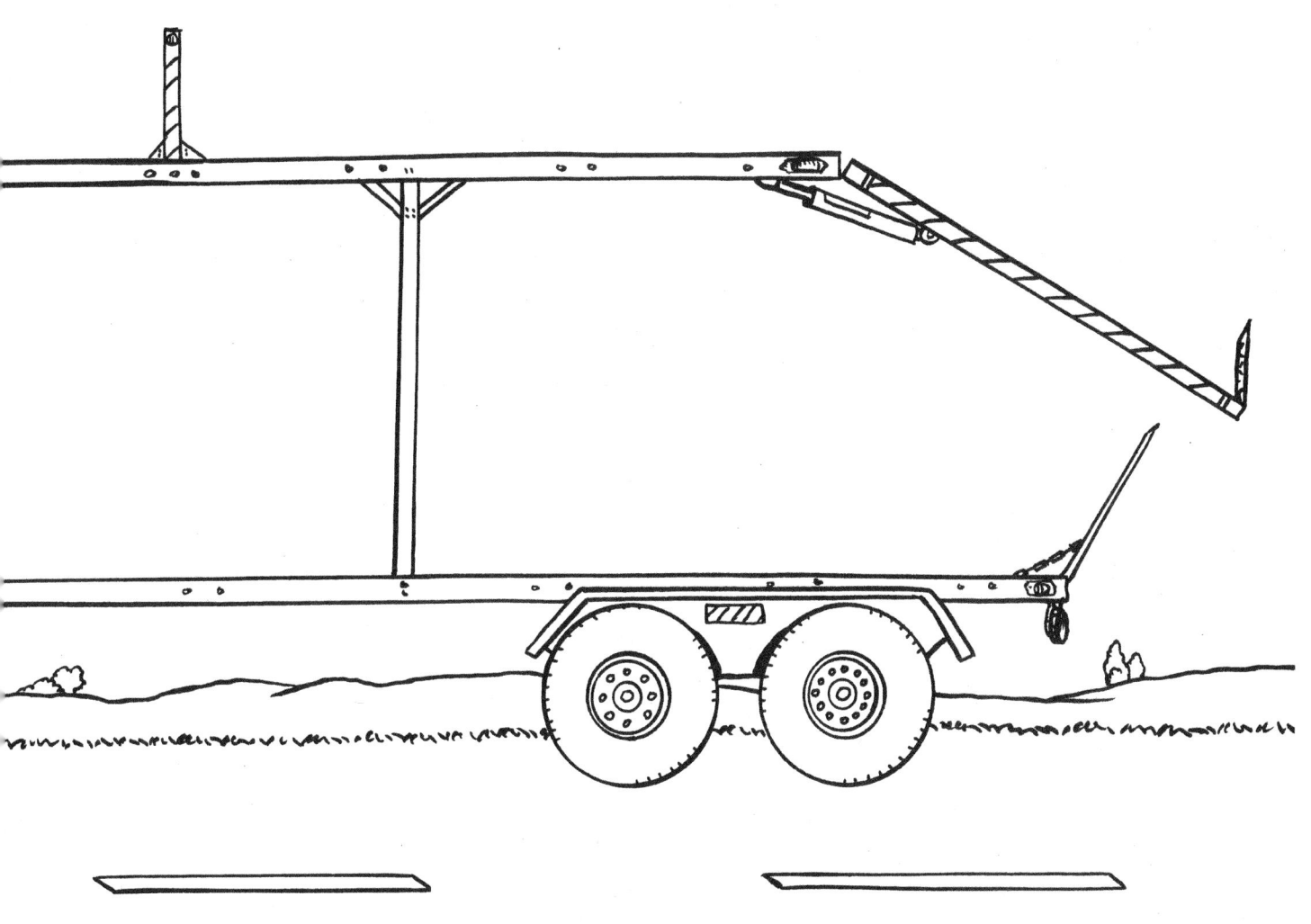

Draw them!

A superhero needs a super ride to do his super good deeds.
Customize it for him.

These mixed-up cars are half old and half new.
Finish the two that are incomplete.

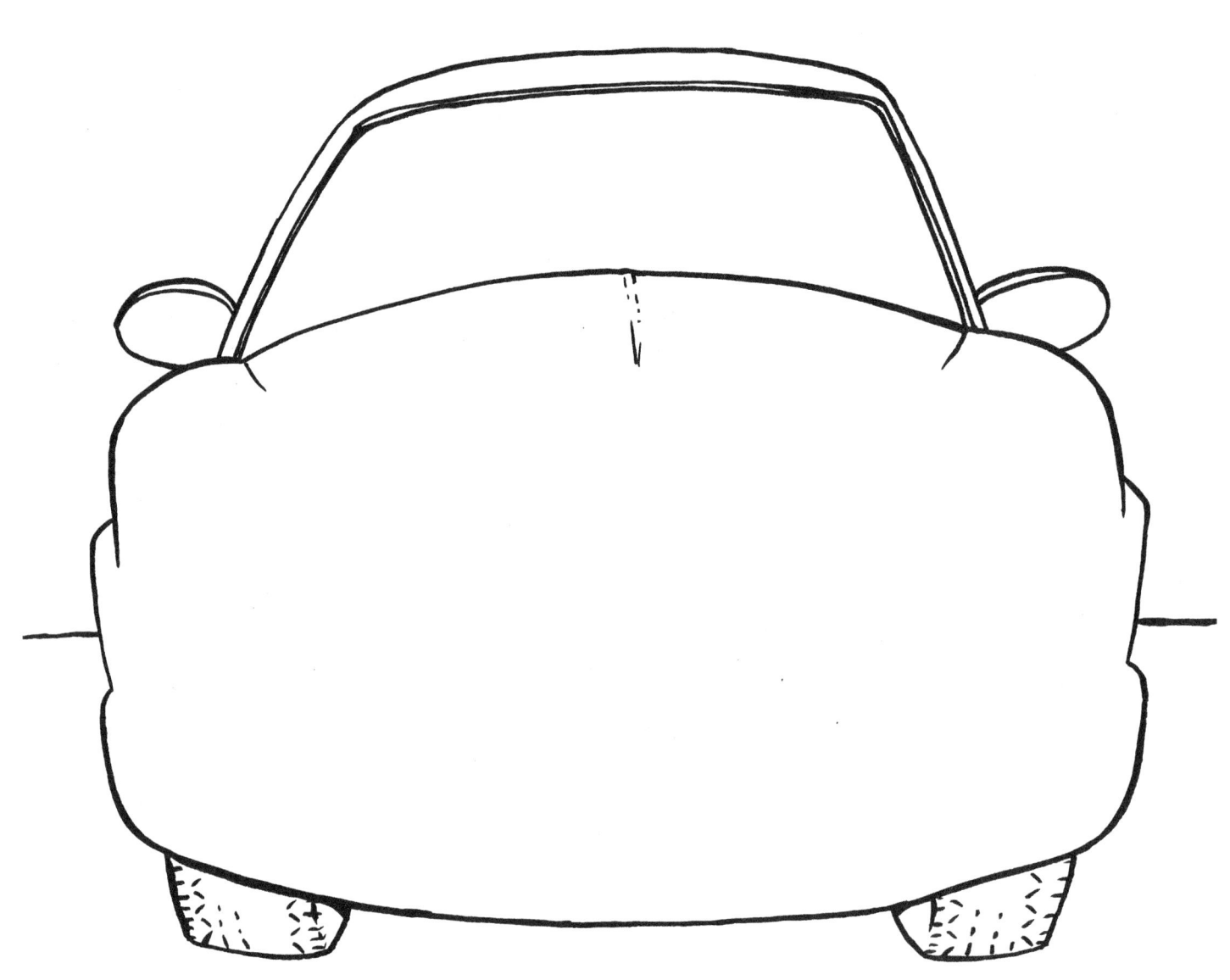

Customize the front end of this ride with a cool grille,
headlights, graphics, and more!

These mixed-up cars are half old and half new.
Finish the two that are incomplete.

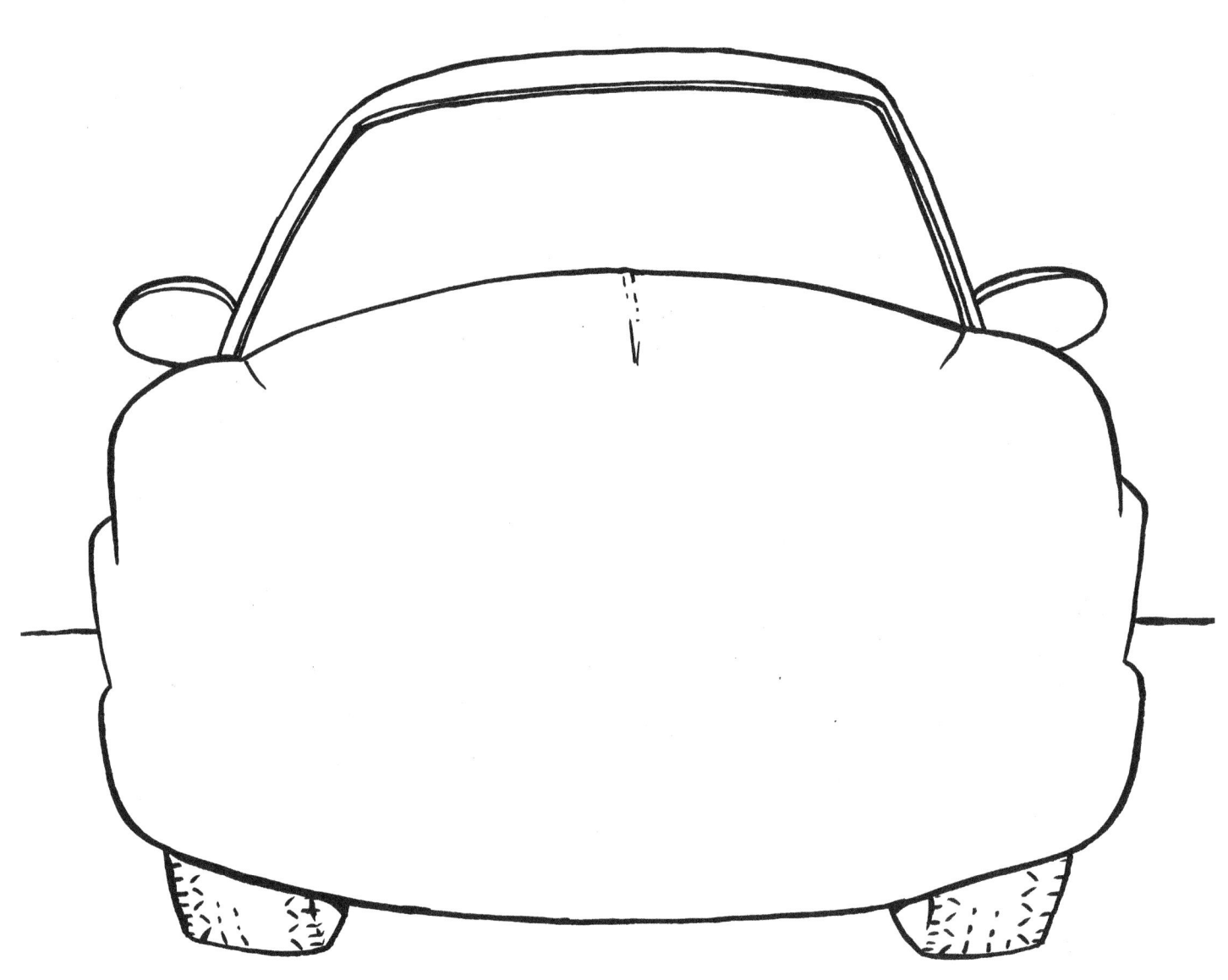

Customize the front end of this ride with a cool grille,
headlights, graphics, and more!

Load the bed of this pick-up truck with
all you need for a day at the beach.

Finish drawing this unique automobile made
entirely out of recycled materials.

A funny man needs a funny car. Draw him a very silly ride!

Two or more cars can fit in this big garage.

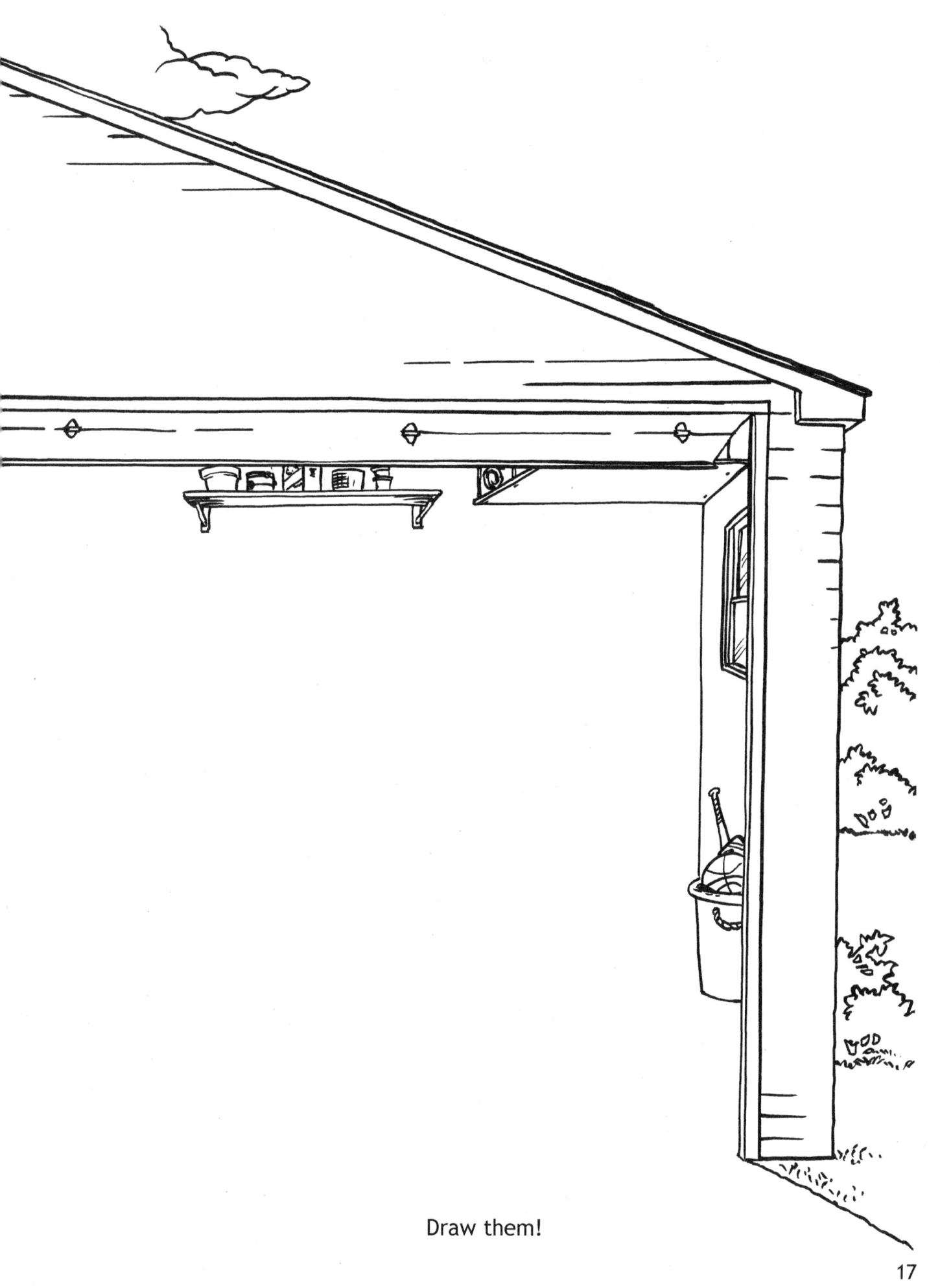

Draw them!

What's on this roadside billboard?

If a dinosaur drove a car, what would it look like?

This racecar is about to cross the finish line.
Give it some cool graphics, sponsor logos, and a number.

You've probably seen a monster truck before,
but what about a monster car?

Give each of these cars a driver behind the wheel.

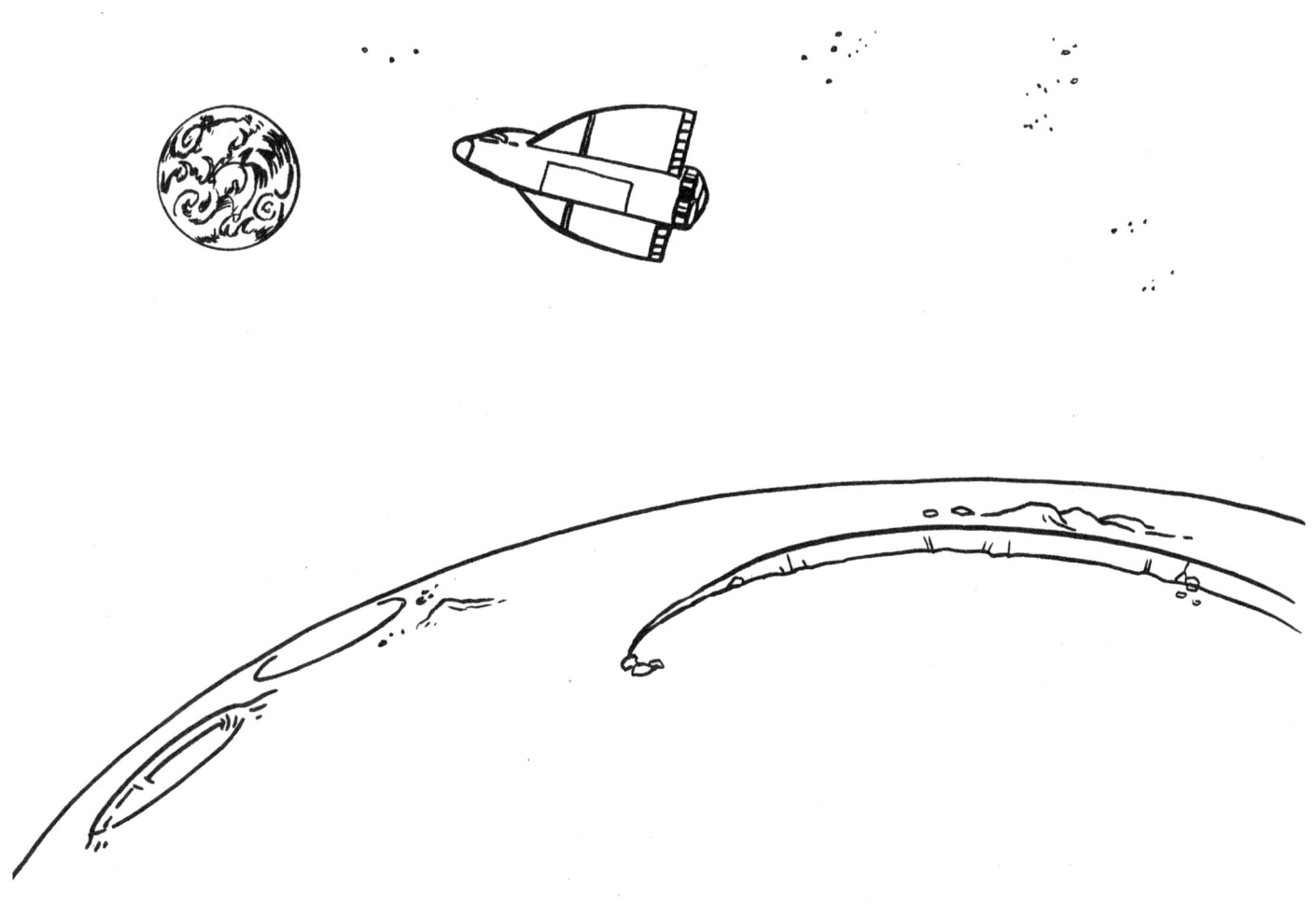

Draw a car that can drive on the moon.
But watch out for those craters!

Are you ready for the "Wild and Wacky Car Race"?

Draw the leading car.

The speeding sports car is no match for this police cruiser!
Draw the coolest cruiser you've ever seen.

What's on these highway road signs?

This taxi is about to take some passengers across the city.
Add some graphics and a cab company logo.

Can you make it to the top of the mountain?
Draw the car that will get you there.

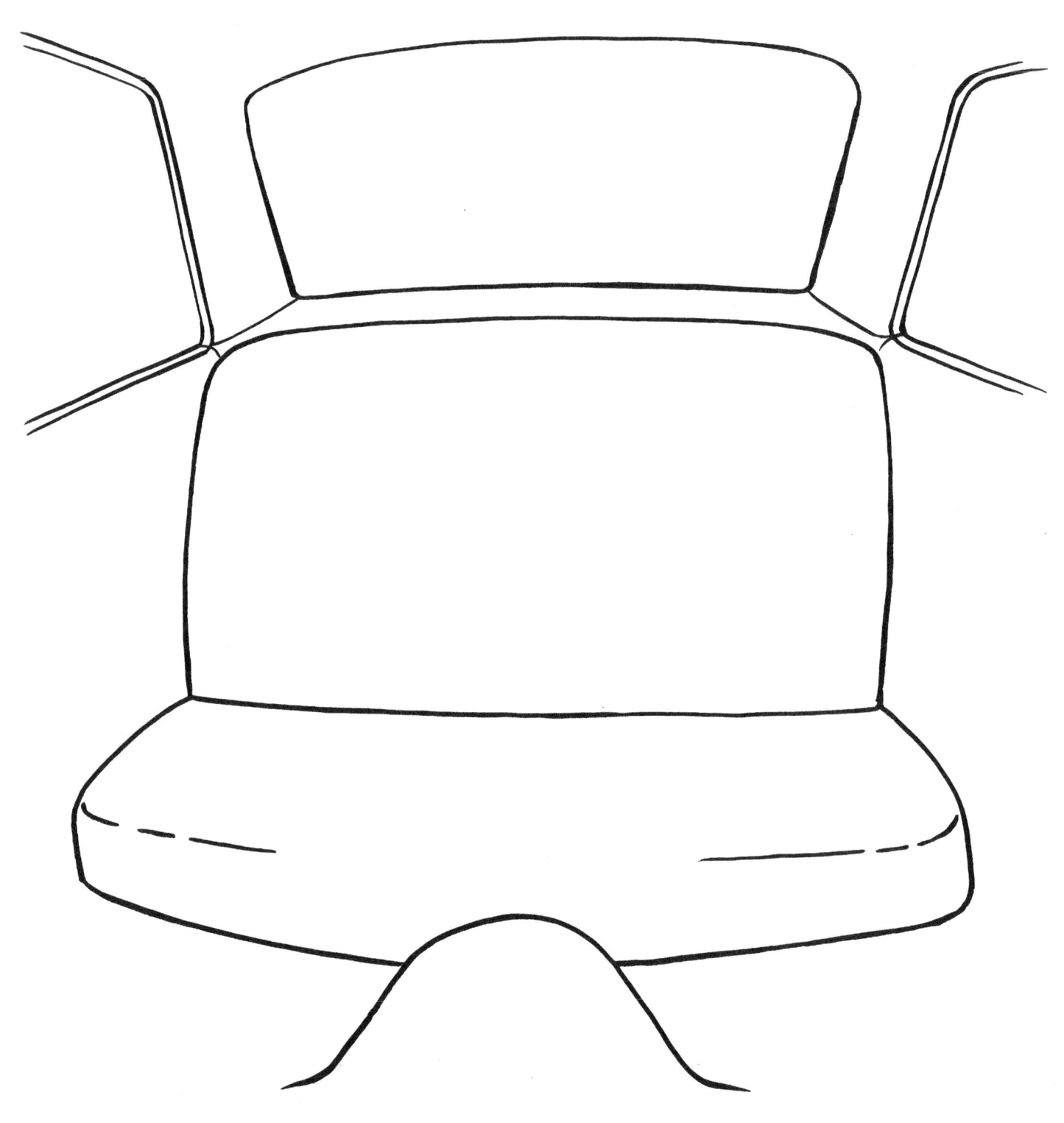

What's in the back seat of your car?

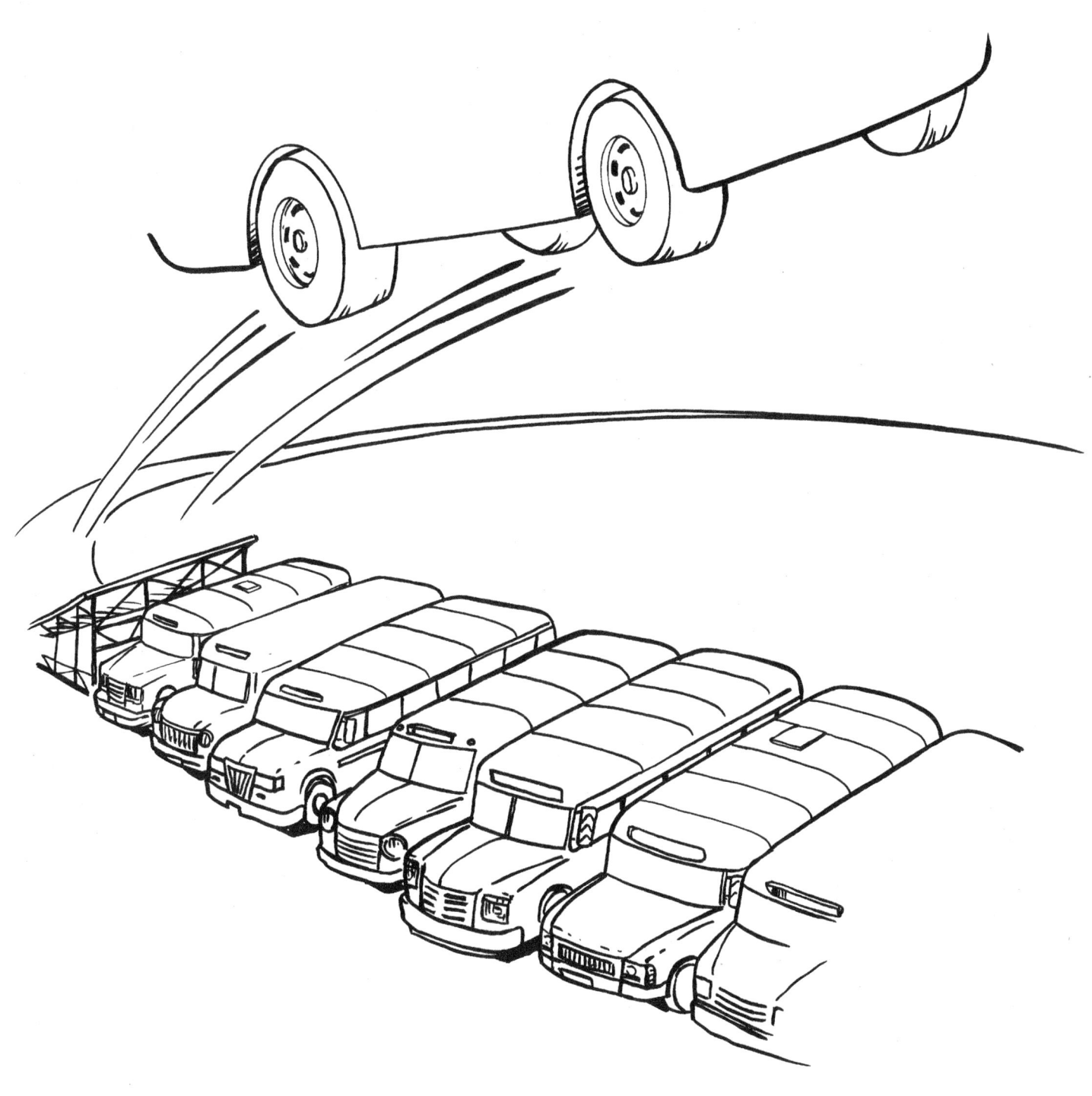

It's a new record! Draw the stunt car that just cleared 7 buses.

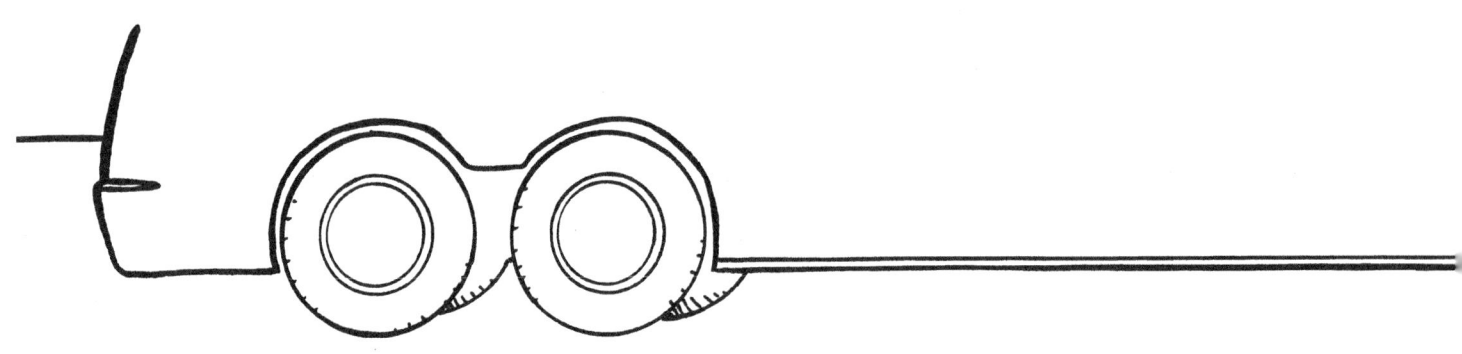

There's a fancy stretch limo waiting outside of your house.

What does it look like?

Cars in the space age will be able to drive *and* fly. Draw one!

Luxury car or sports car? This couple wants the
coolest ride to get them around town.

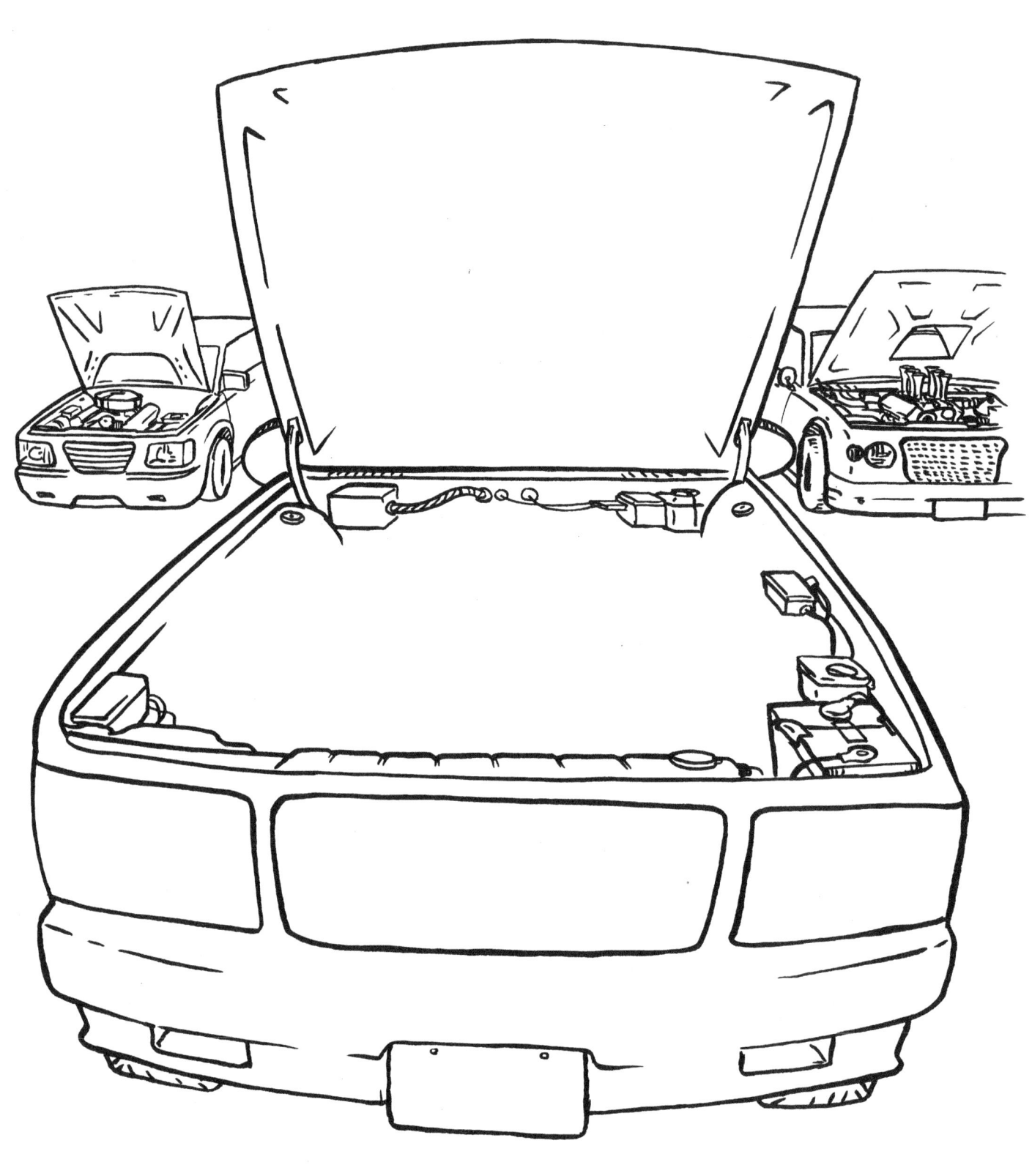

There's a lot of power under this hood. Draw the engine.

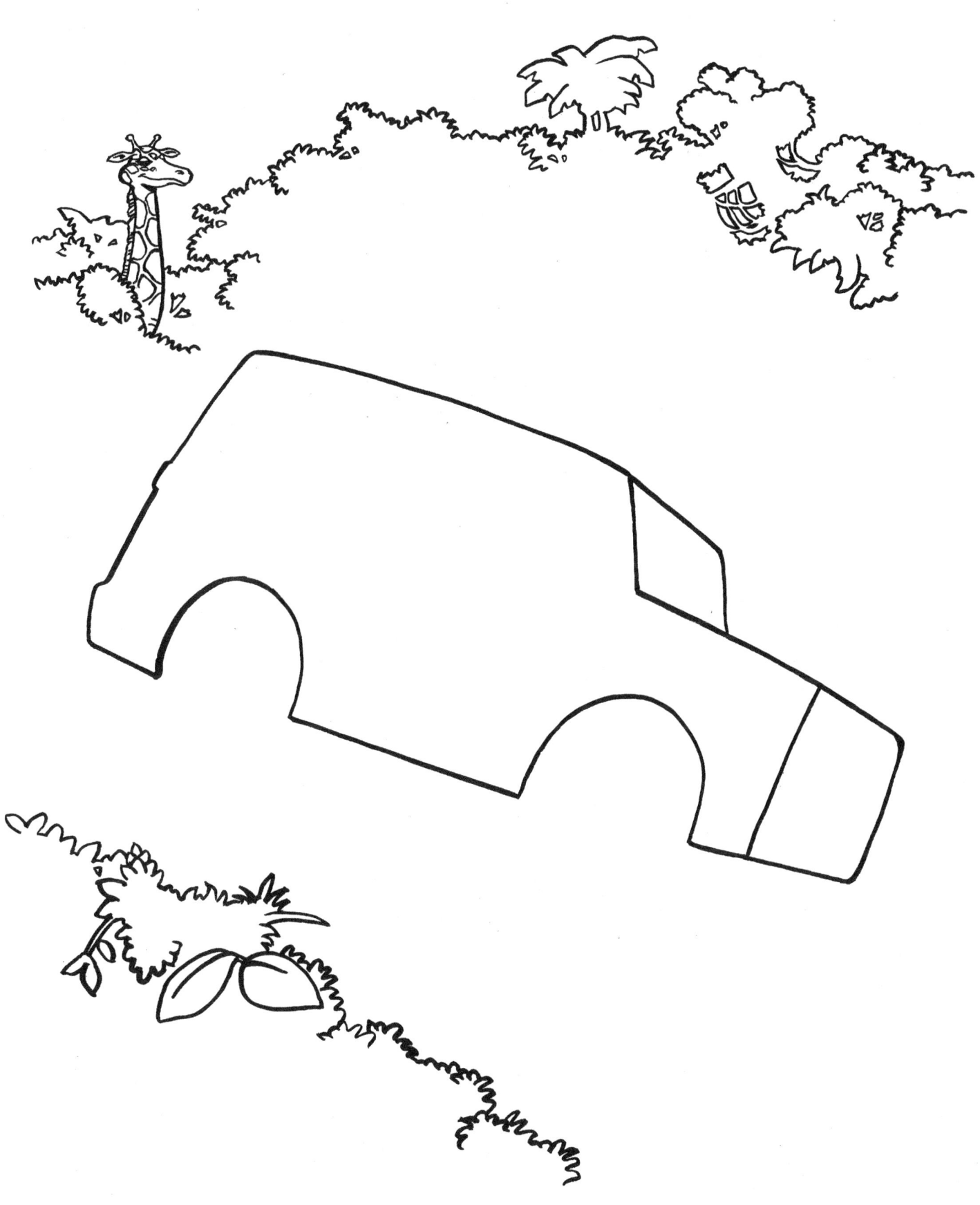

Set this car up with all the gear it needs for a jungle safari.

Add more cars to the celebrity's exotic car collection.

What's in your glove compartment?

Traffic jam!

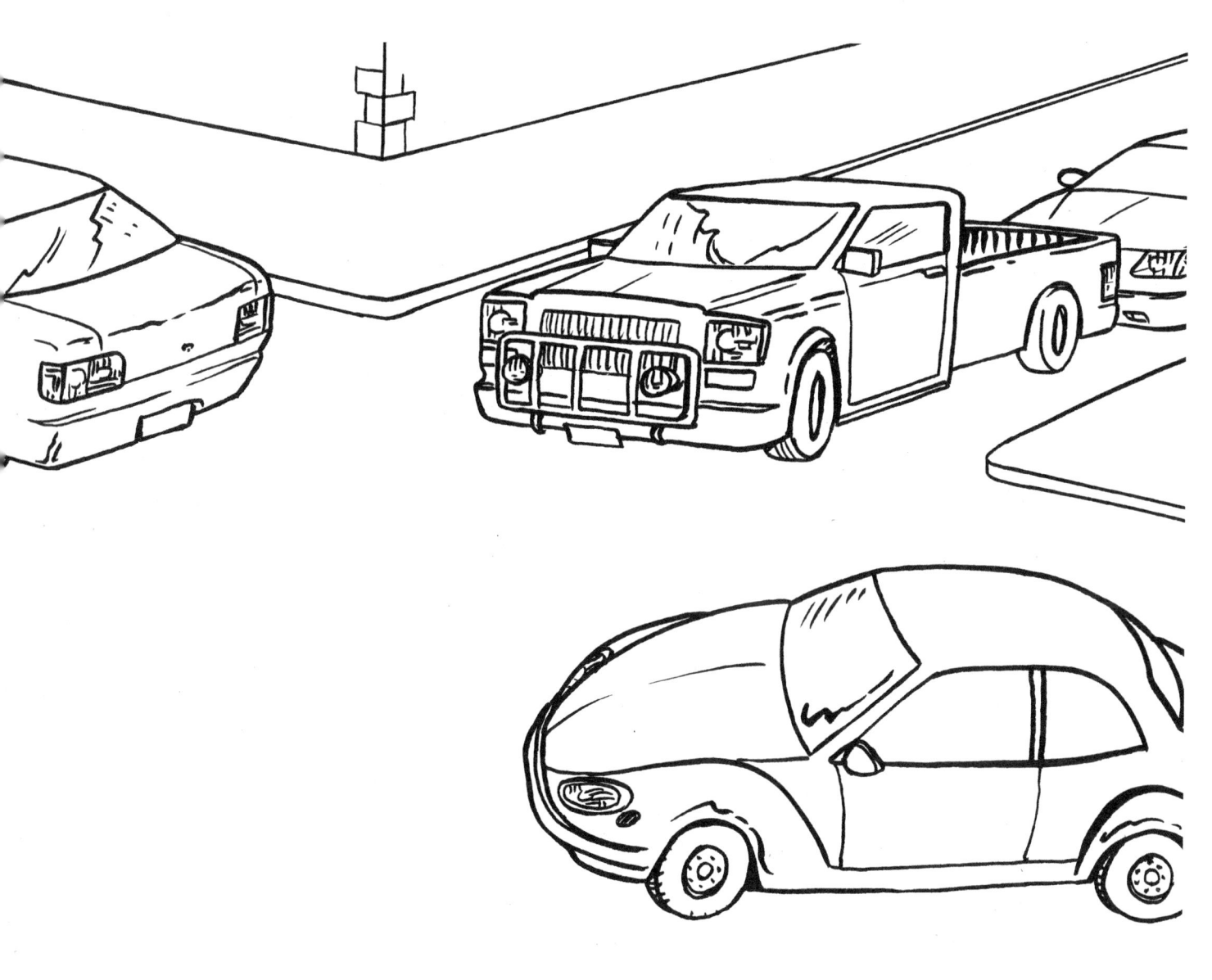

Fill the street with cars moving in every direction.

The gardener packed the park van with all his tools.
Fill it with rakes, shovels, and other materials.

Zoom! Draw the leading contestant in the minivan race.

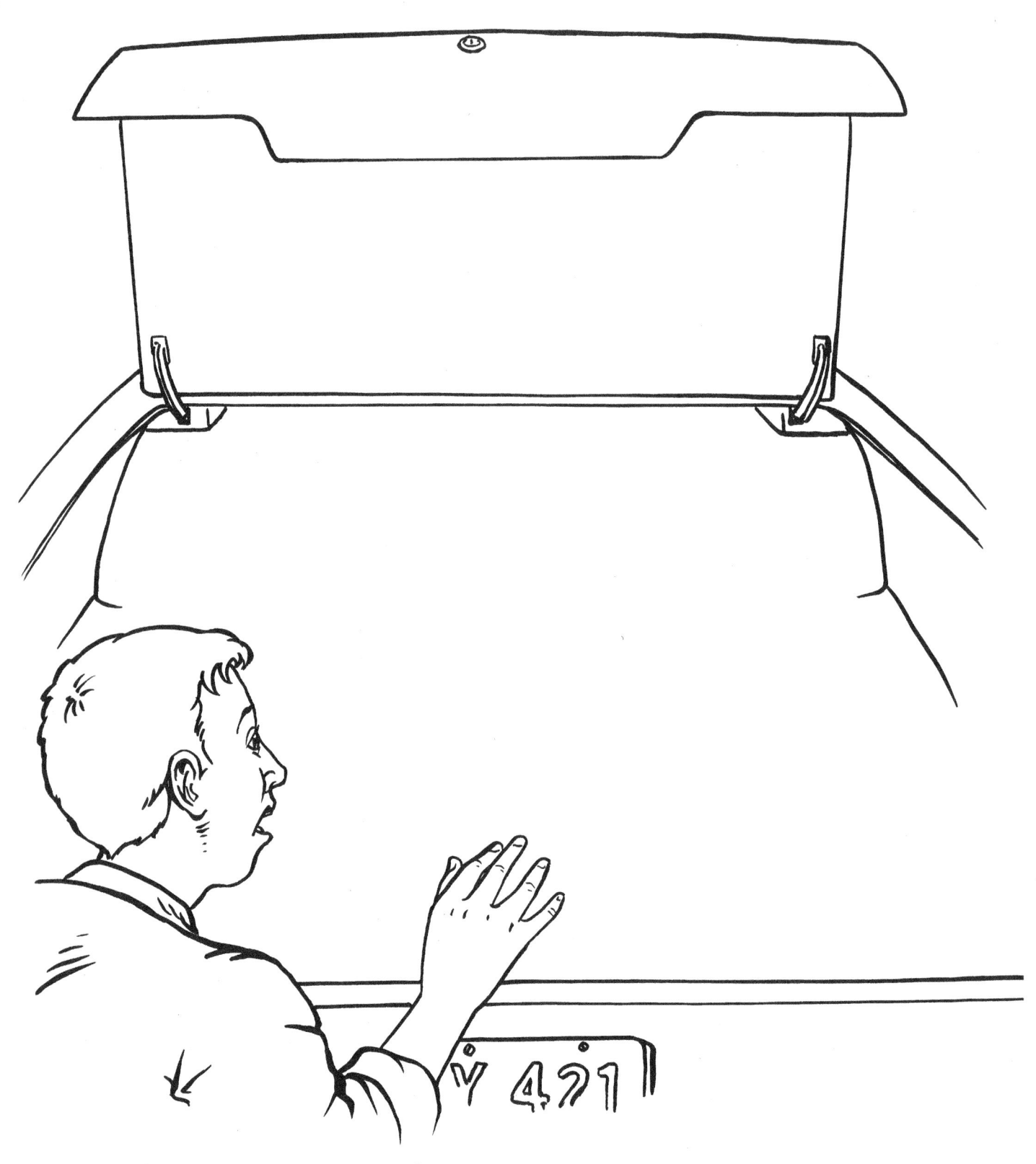

What's in your trunk?

This car has seen better days.
Draw a vehicle that really belongs in the junkyard.

Draw yourself and a friend in the front seats of this cool car.

Boo! Draw some ghostly spirits in the ghostly car by the haunted house.

Draw the winner of the demolition derby.

This car purrs like a kitten!
Design this ride for the cat-lover and his feline friends.

Cover the back of the minivan in cool bumper stickers.

What's on your license plate?

Start your engines! Design the cars competing in the race.

Draw a pile of old cars at the impound lot.

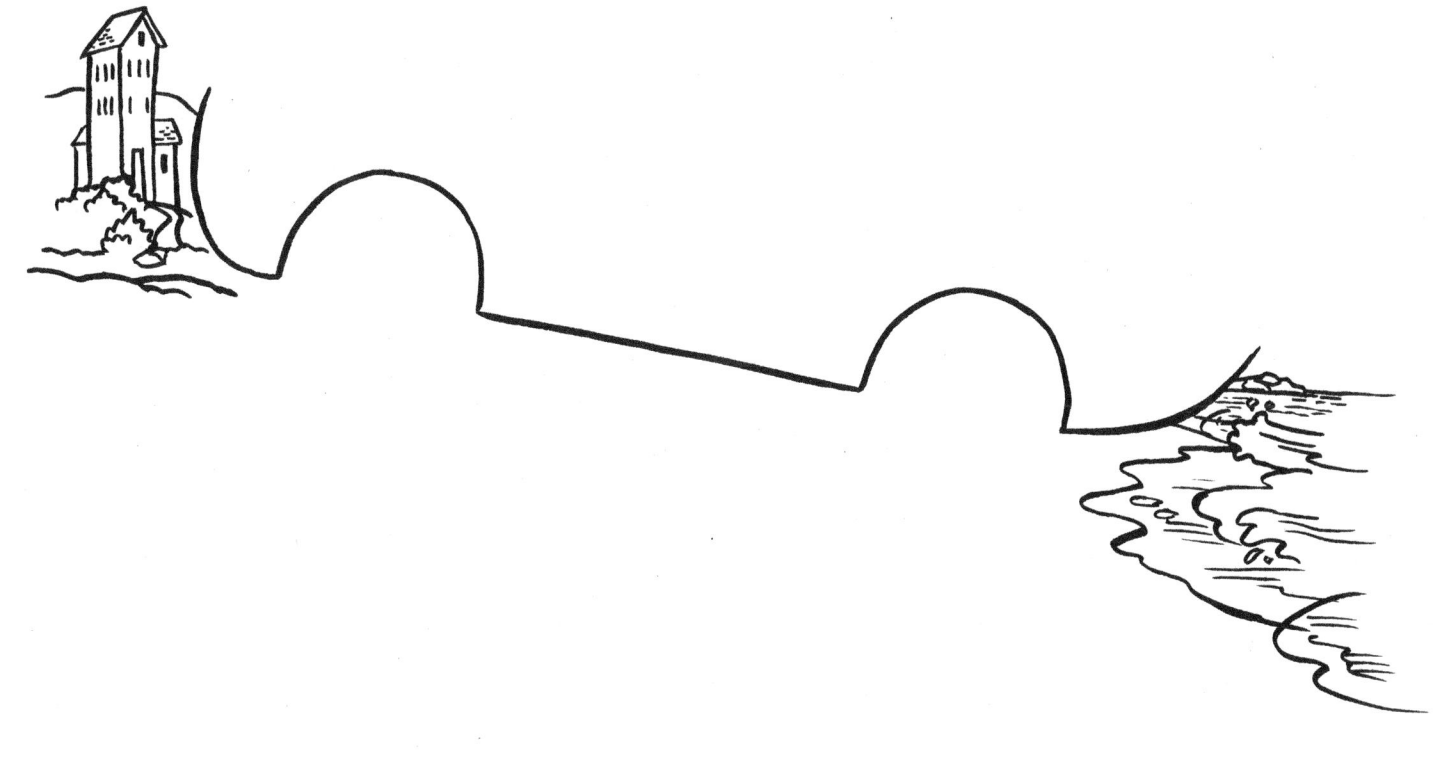

Imagine a car that could travel on land and in the water.
What would it look like?

Draw the off-road vehicle leading this bumpy race.

Draw your own addition to the hotrod show.

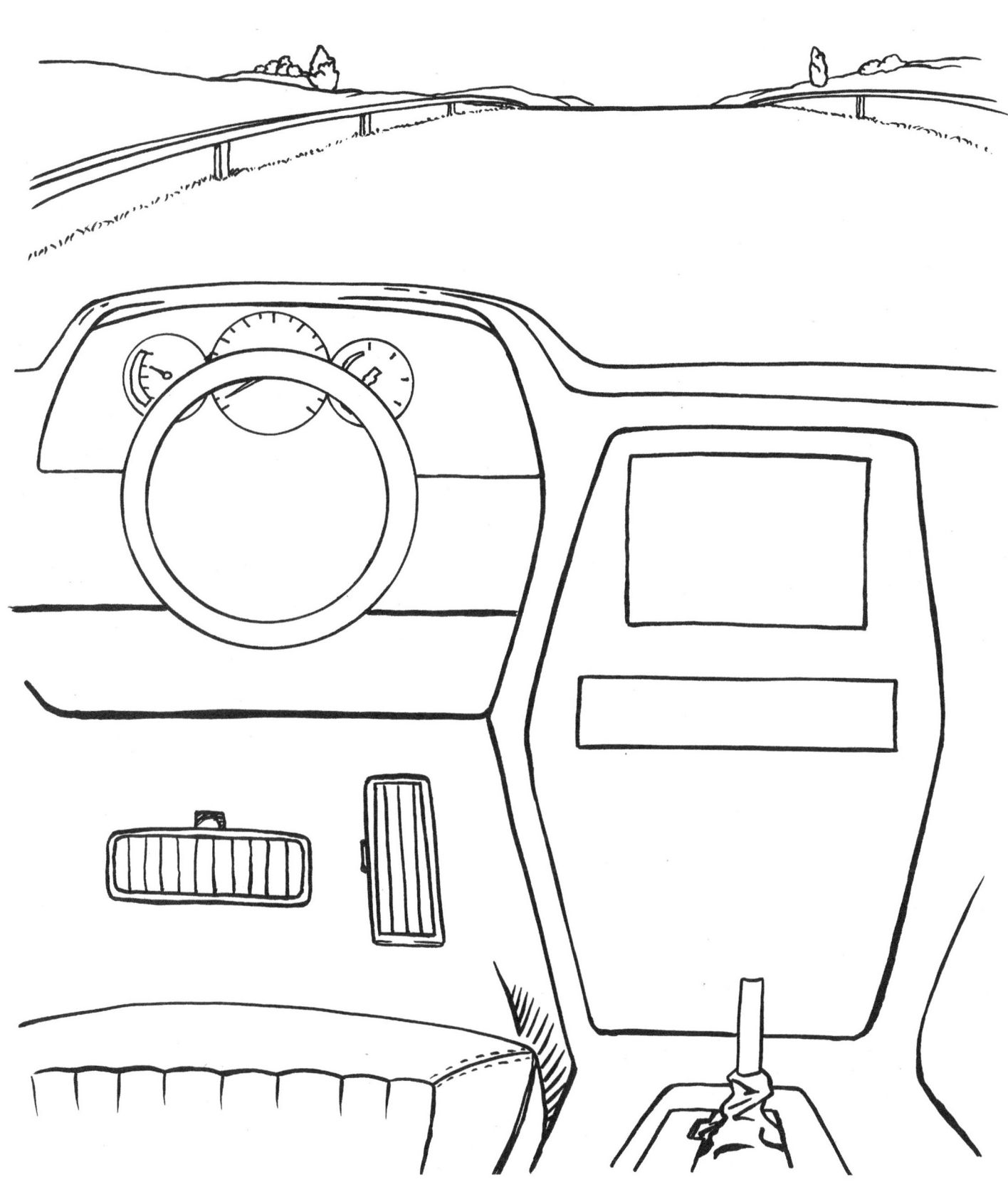

Design a cool dashboard for this car.
Add a steering wheel, radio, and more.

You've got the green light!

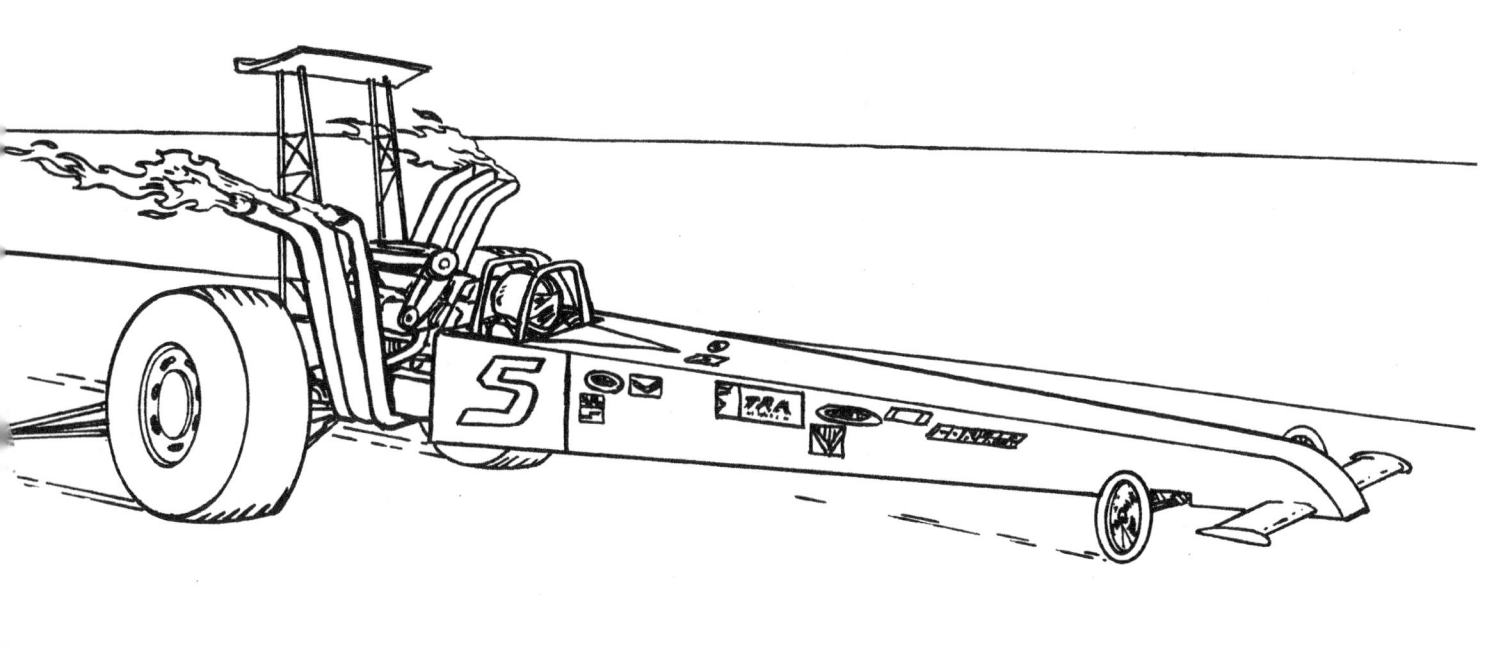

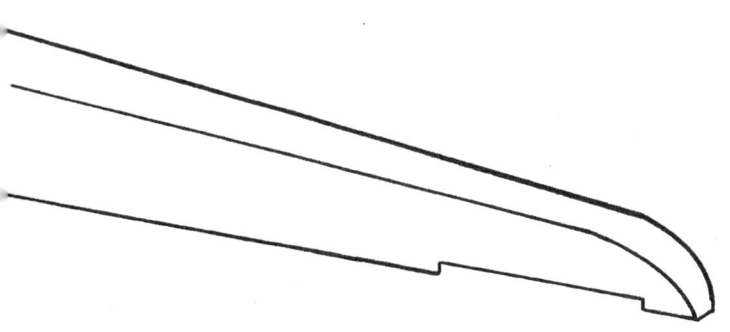

Finish the dragster speeding down the strip.

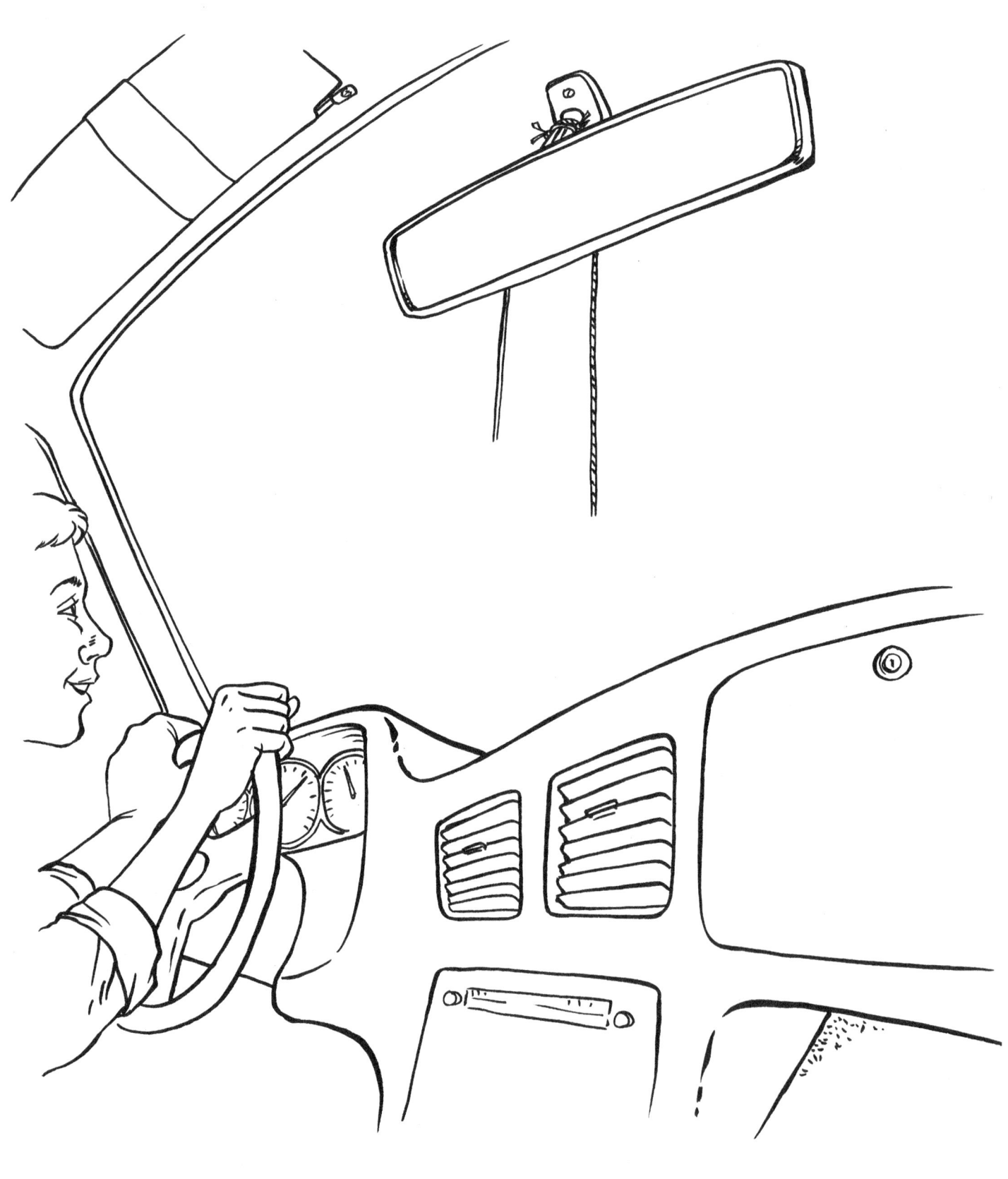

What's hanging from your rearview mirror?